Frugal Yankee Guide

to

Supermarkets

Frugal Yankee Guides, number 1

Garen Daly and Louise Reilly Sacco

Frugal Yankee Press

Frugal Yankee Press
73 Parker Road
Needham MA 02494
www.FrugalYankee.com

Summary: "Practical, actionable ideas to get the most for your money in today's supermarkets." – provided by the publisher

ISBN-13: 978-1456569051
ISBN-10: 1456569058

Contents

BEING A
FRUGAL YANKEE

A Frugal Yankee is smart and thrifty.

The day the colonists landed at Plymouth Rock, New Englanders became Frugal Yankees. They have held on to the old or adopted the new simply to better themselves and the families' lives. They were curious and intelligent, with a strong skepticism. They knew how to make a buck and how to make that buck last. They passed this tradition down and created a culture of finding real value for the real world. By adopting this ethos, they became world leaders in business, culture and politics.

Today chattering advertising, focus group marketing and unbridled consumerism have challenged this tradition.

Just when we thought consumerism might trump wisdom, a new breed of Frugal Yankee emerged. They see beyond the 'shop til you drop' mentality. They are not always New Englanders, but are dedicated to that simple New England proposition - value. When money is spent, it better be a good deal and even better value.

This is where Garen Daly and Louise Reilly Sacco come in. They aren't cheap or penny pinchers. They want their money's worth. To do that, they use all the tools available: web searches, experts and even the wisdom of an octogenarian farmer. These Frugal Yankees explore old-fashioned values to solve today's problems.

In their first book, they offer an overview of food shopping, the most basic of family chores. Americans spend over $7,000 a year to feed a small family. Now toss in that food prices are expected to rise at least 4% this year. Knowing the ins and outs of supermarkets is a good step to feed your family well AND save some money, money that can be used for something else, like medical bills, travel or education.

In future books they will tackle additional topics. Each book will be dedicated to finding value, saving money and still enjoying life, the Frugal Yankee way.

THE SUPERMARKET

It's basic.

Families need food. Without it, we die. It is more primary than even procreation. Adults secure food for themselves, their children and maybe others in their community. We do it. Our parents did it. Their parents did it. Our earliest ancestors did it by hunting or gathering.

Today we have a societal agreement that someone else will do the hunting, the gathering, the farming, or the slaughtering. This food is brought to us and stored in a convenient place. From time to time, we go and buy what we need. That's the deal and it works well.

This book explores how this works, how it has gotten sophisticated, how it uses tricks to get you to spend more and strategies for you to navigate an increasingly opaque system.

First rule: understand today's grocery store isn't the grocery store you grew up with. Today's supermarkets and superstores offer an ever growing selection of food and merchandise. These are separated into more and more departments in larger and larger stores. Economies of scale can make the prices seem excellent, but many times they are not what they seem.

Second rule: remember, supermarkets don't sell food. They sell real estate. How things are laid in a store comes after intensive study of human psychology. How many of us have heard that milk is placed to make shoppers walk past aisles and aisles of other foods in the hope they will buy something besides a quart of milk? That's just the tip of the iceberg.

Going back to that 'real estate' concept, have you ever wondered why certain products are at eye level in the center of an aisle? That's primo location and you can bet your winning lottery ticket that access to that space is negotiated.

Third rule: although the supermarket isn't your enemy it will take advantage of you. The big companies running today's stores are not altruistic. They want to make as much money as they can. Food is a product to be sold. We shoppers have money and they want as much as we'll give them. Today's supermarket shopper needs to be well informed and to use this information wisely. That should be the new contract - I'll give you money, but only if I can find healthy food for my family at a very reasonable price.

That's what this book is all about.

IN THE BEGINNING

The modern supermarket got its start during The Great Depression (1931-1939). Price sensitivity was at its peak. Stores learned that by offering a wider selection of food at lower prices, customers would abandon old ways of shopping and adopt news ones. This concept caught on, and quickly. Growth was accelerated as the huge post-World War II demographic shifted out of the cities to the new suburbs. This marked the beginning of the Baby Boom phenomena. The mobility afforded by cars plus cheap land made this shift dramatic and culturally significant. Supermarkets followed suit. In the suburbs they could expand beyond the traditional cramped urban floor plan. Stores went from 6,000 square feet and grew to 12,000. As years passed, supermarket size continued to expand. Today a supermarket runs about 45, 000 square feet.

The first supermarket was created by Clarence Saunders in 1916. His Piggly Wiggly store in Memphis TN was the first self-serve grocery store. Early supermarkets did not offer meat and fresh produce

As the supermarket industry matured, growth slowed. To maintain profits, the industry began to focus less on building growth and more on maximizing per shopper sales.

Tricks to increase impulse buying or to sell more high profit items began in earnest. Product placement became a science backed by focus groups and human behavioral testing.

This constantly evolving body of knowledge that has spawned ubiquitous use of 'loyalty' cards and now smart phone technology adding another layer away to traditional food shopping.

The edge has shifted away from the shopper in favor of the conglomerates.

They are not evil. It is a case where they place profits over the needs of their customers.

The Frugal Yankee wants to level the playing field. We will explain old and new techniques used by the industry. This makes it easier to strategize grocery shopping by taking advantage of their techniques to save money and feed quality food to your family.

For the Frugal Yankee, it is rarely about the cheapest price. It's about getting true value, just like those Frugal Yankees of yore.

The average person walks about 90 steps per minute By slowing the tempo stores slow that pace, giving more time for impulse shopping. One report showed when German music is played, people buy German wine, switch to French music, French wine

THE SEDUCTION

Supermarkets are just businesses trying to make a profit. They have been remarkably successful. Their success means more foods at lower costs than at any time in history. Today's family takes less time to earn money for food than ever. Americans spend a smaller percent of total income on food than most other nations. This is attributed to lower food costs, better distribution and economies of size. It is classic American capitalism at its best.

Capitalism has a downside.

The drive for profits created an American diet that is unhealthful. There are too many foods at convenient prices with too many calories, too much fat or too much sodium. The result is a diet of unbalanced nutrition.

We have been seduced by the food industry.

The allure of cheap food comes with a price. This time it is our health.

Supermarkets and even convenience stores learned a long time ago that placing candy, soda, chips, donuts etc, near the exit spurs sales. These impulse items make more profit than apples and carrots.

They also learned that the more they stock, the more they sell. Hey, perhaps that explains the aisles devoted to chips, crackers and cookies while eggs have a small corner of the diary section.

Over time, supermarket operators became more sophisticated. Aisles became "shopper environments". They tweak the environment based on the latest behavioral studies. Lighting is adjusted to augment sales. Aromas wafting from a bakery increase sales. Every aspect of the environment is studied, tweaked and altered with one goal - more sales. Stimulate the senses, the pocketbook opens.

There isn't much beyond boycotting a store a shopper can do to eliminate these temptations. Knowing the tricks makes us better, more value-driven shoppers. Value is what a Frugal Yankee strives for.

LOYALTY: A ONE WAY STREET

A recent supermarket message is: "Become a regular customer and we'll give you special privileges. We'll call it a Loyalty Card."

Sounds like a good idea?

Customers get special prices, customized coupons and a summary of savings. What could be wrong with this?

Lots.

First, the systems to support the Loyalty Cards costs money. So it is no surprise that studies find supermarkets without loyalty cards have lower overall prices even when factoring in the 'deals' offered by the cards

Like the magician who uses misdirection, stores use misdirection to increase profits at the shopper's expense. The deals, coupons and other 'bennies' offered, are easily offset by higher prices.

Second, understand the loyalty card system captures, tracks, and analyzes all data. The data is used to understand consumer behavior and maximize profits as they build a profile of your shopping habits. Also you're paying for it.

On top of that, the loyalty card system works with partnered companies. Using the shopper profile, they tailor specials to sell more targeted products. For example, someone buying salsa gets a coupon for chips. They steer the shopper towards higher profit items. You spend more. They make more.

This technique is growing with new technologies like smart phones. Smart phone scanning and couponing allows manufacturers to offer coupons at the buying decision point, not at the cash register. Using the salsa example, with new *calculate as you go apps*, a shopper scans an item into their cell phone. Immediately a coupon for chips appears on the cell phone. Impulse buying accomplished.

How effective are these and other *loyalty card* techniques?

A study compared loyalty card supermarkets to traditional low priced stores. The card holding shoppers spent 42% more on groceries, motivated by the belief they are saving money or getting good deals.

Check out this disturbing aspect of loyalty cards. They discriminate against the poor. To help pay for this 'service', stores compensate with increased prices elsewhere, usually staples. The less affluent, who are restricted by location and means, end up paying more for their basics.

Perhaps the most troubling issue is simply who owns all that information gleaned from using the cards. It isn't you. It is them. They own it. They can use it, sell it, or even lose it. Do you want your HMO to know how many six packs you buy or ice cream or chips? Do you want some hacker to slip by firewall and steal your personal information?

If there's only one grocery store nearby, most of us will use a loyalty card. But be disciplined. Don't be lured to buy things you don't want or need. Remember, most stores will give you those prices anyway. Just ask at the register and they'll scan a store card.

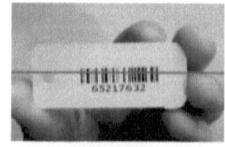

BIG PICTURE

Debunking myths and offering guidance.

ORGANIC & FAIR TRADE is not to be trusted. It isn't a rip-off, but it isn't what you think either.

Traditionally supermarkets show single digit percentage growth. The 'organic' foods market has been growing at 12-14% per year. Any smart business can see the trend. Families want healthier food. They are willing to pay, too. As a result, supermarkets are demanding and getting foods that are 'organic'.

TOSS THAT SALAD - Germs can grow with abandon at salad bars. Hot food requires a constant 135° to remain safe. Fresh foods require 41° or lower to keep germs from growing. If one or the other isn't being met, food could go bad. Be careful.

There is a catch.

Organic conjures an image of food grown without pesticides, using natural fertilizers and grown on small, family farms. Healthy food as if our grandparents grew it.

For the food industry, organic is a mass produced product adhering to standards they created. It isn't from a small farm. It is what lawyers, legislators and accountants define as organic. Be careful with organic food. Organic, or even natural does not mean "good". Arsenic is a natural mineral, but it isn't good for you. The word is a blurry marketing term.

The bottom line is simple. Decide if the price premium is justified. Just because that bag of chips says organic, it doesn't mean it is good for you. So be smart, be savvy and don't get suckered by the marketing.

MOMMY, MOMMY, PLEEEEASE is a refrain heard too often in a store. Those very smart people who are trying to get you to spend more money know kids influence buying. The items designed to appeal to a child's taste are purposely stocked at their eye level. Recently, some stores have begun to put candy near cereals. Now that's a health message.

Set rules down before the cookie-inspired melt down. Incentives work. If the child helps with the shopping, allow them to select, say, their favorite cereal. Of course, bad behavior would negate that.

Get the kids involved. Send them off to get one or two items, cereal, flour, something easy to find. Teach them how to locate and understand unit pricing and why items are where they are on shelves. They learn to shop, find good deals and help the family.

Oh yeah, one last word of advice, be careful at the checkout. The chance for impulse buying - magazines and goodies - is high. Why do you think they have so many 'goodies' there? Stay firm. No whining or begging at the checkout.

END OF AISLE displays are associated in our minds with good deals, but be leery. Far too many are not sale items. This is just another trick. The cluttered bargain bin is calculated for effect, not price. It may be a sale item, but more often than not, the real deals are found elsewhere

STORES HAVE PERSONALITY and have strengths and weaknesses. For example, a big box store is good for basic weekly or bi-weekly groceries; a drugstore chain for health and beauty products; a farmstand for produce; and maybe a second big grocery store to skim off their specials. Specialty stores may work into the mix: Trader Joe's for good prices on a limited range of high quality products; BJs or Costco to stock up.

STOCKING UP

STOCKING UP is a key to spending less. Tying up money in bargain groceries is a great investment. This depends on having sufficient space. Most families can find a shelf in a basement, garage, or closet to store staples, paper goods and cleaning supplies. Filling a freezer helps it operate more efficiently.

When you see a great price, estimate what your family uses, how much storage space you have, and how long you want to stock up for. Remember many store specials go in 3 month cycles. It's likely that there'll be another great price.

Nearly every store advertises weekly specials. Many are *loss leaders*, on which the store loses money. They plan on shoppers coming in for the specials, then buying more. There are shoppers who go to two or three grocery stores each week to stock up on specials. Most of us are not ready for this investment in time and gas.

It's not hard to check two or three stores and note prices on things you buy regularly. Then decide which is best. Shoppers who have several stores around may be willing to make a second stop sometimes for advertised specials. If there's another store near your workplace or a regular driving route, it's easy get in and out quickly with the specials.

Use the warehouse stores like Costco or BJs the same way. Know the regular prices. Consider those giant packs only if you'll really save money and if you'll use the product up before the expiration date. Remember that "sell by" is not the same as "use by".

The trap with warehouse stores is that it's easy to be lured into buying things you don't need, are not good for you, or weren't in your plan. Think carefully if you want three pounds of cashews in the cupboard, even though the price is great and they are delicious!

Sometimes you'll have to repackage when you get home. If you find a really good deal on chicken quarters, go ahead and buy that enormous 'family pack'. When you get home, separate, wrap in aluminum foil and freezer bags, label and freeze until you need it.

A word about expiration dates, stickers on fresh food and meat say "BEST IF USED BY". It is a suggestion, not a law. The Feds regulate some products, but not all. So be savvy. Use your senses. If it looks bad or smells bad, don't buy it.

The 'SELL-BY' date is also not a law; it is an internal store guideline. The 'sell-by' means 'how long it may be displayed'. If it can be sold until this date, it's safe to eat for at least days after that as long as it's stored properly.

A good resource for understanding what these terms mean for different categories of foods can be found at: http://www.fsis.usda.gov/factsheets/food_product_dating/index.asp

PLAN OF ATTACK

OK, you've read how a Frugal Yankee thinks about
supermarkets. Short of going
off 'the grid', growing your
own food, slaughtering your
own meat and never setting
foot in a supermarket again,
you'll be making a trip to one
soon. Depending on the size
of your family, you could
easily spend up to $10,000 a
year on groceries. To be
practical, save money and
take advantage of what they
offer, you need a plan of
attack. Like any plan, it
requires discipline and
intelligence to work. The
following is the Frugal Yankee way.

MAKE A LIST

Keep a pad or white board in your kitchen. As you run out
or think of needs, write it down. Train your family to do the
same. This will make shopping easier and more efficient.

We like to recycle incoming envelopes. Write the list on the
back and put coupons inside. Browse the weekly grocery flier
and add specials or more menu ideas.

HAVE A BUDGET

Do it and stick to it. Decide BEFORE you go how much to
spend. Discipline works.

Too often when we hit the supermarket, the surrounding temptations win. The rationalizations begin. By the time you get to the check out, the shopping cart has fancy cheeses, top shelf breads, the finest meat and the most expensive wine. Bingo! The trip to the store has blown your budget to bits. So stay strong, stick with the plan.

THE BASICS

Build your list around the basics. Look at the circulars for loss leaders and seasonal deals. Plan meals accordingly. Check your cabinets for staple supplies. Anything additional, including treats, are decided in your kitchen, not in the supermarket.

Look at your list and figure out if you have any coupon. See page 21 our separate section on coupons and how to use them effectively.

CONVENIENCE, HARDLY

Suppose you buy one can of tuna a week at $1.59. If it goes on sale for $1.29, you can buy 20 cans, after checking the "sell by" date.

You invest $25.80 for something that would cost $31.80. You saved $6. Your return on investment is 23% for 20 weeks, or about 58% a year.

That's a darn good ROI - return on investment, better than most.

When planning meals, don't think convenience foods. One study found that many of these foods take as long to prepare as a real meal. Also they cost more. Their ingredients are suspect. They probably have more salt, fat or sugar in them than you want. There is a reason they are called convenience foods, but convenient for whom?

WASTE NOT, WANT NOT

It's an old saying that still rings true, waste not, want not. Analyzing your food consumption and knowing what is being thrown away will save money.

Milk going sour? Fruits rotting? Science experiments getting fuzzy in the fridge? Often this is the result of poor planning.

There are two ways to solve this. First, don't buy as much. For example, milk is cheaper by the gallon, but nothing is saved if 25% goes bad. Buying half gallons will save in the long run.

Second, think ahead. Use leftover foods creatively. Plan for their use in your regular menus. For example, take wilted celery, and some other past their prime veggies, toss them into a big pot, throw spices in and make vegetable stock. Then freeze the stock for future soups and stews. Tips like these abound. The old standard cookbooks like *Joy of Cooking* is full of them.

NEVER SHOP HUNGRY

We all know the story about the stoners who go to a supermarket hungry. They buy nothing but junk food and lots of it. Similarly, going to the store hungry will result in buying things not really needed and perhaps even bad for you. The aromas, the displays, the desires can easily overwhelm your better senses. Simple rule. Don't shop hungry

SHOP ALONE

This can be a tough for families, but if you can swing it, go solo. It'll make the trip go faster, with fewer distractions and no temptations from nagging voices. If you can't do it alone, develop strategies to help. Shop with a friend and split the shopping duties. You get this, I'll get that. Failing that, have the kids help as we talked about that earlier.

But it gets down to this. Temptations and distractions can take away from the task, focusing on getting the most food for your money and the best quality for your family.

BASKET CASE STRATEGY

Any shopping strategy should include effective use of the tools at hand, for example shopping cart versus carry basket.

The standard routine is to grab a cart and work your way through the aisles. If you're getting only a few items, take a carry basket instead. That'll lessen the chance of filling the cart up with things you don't need.

Here's another trick, leave the cart at the end of the aisle. Walk from one end to another picking up items in your arms. Impulse buying will be inhibited by your full arms, and you will be able to maneuver more freely around the other carts. This makes for a quicker, more efficient shopping trip.

BUY IN BULK

Economies of scale are usually smart shopping. Unit prices are better, less packaging and in general, a better deal.

Here is a little know fact, many supermarkets will rotate the items they place on sale according time of year and other factors. The usual separation between sales is 13 weeks. Start tracking those items your family uses, and how often they go on sale. Buy in bulk accordingly.

THE SKINNY
ON SALES

ADVERTISED SPECIALS are usually "loss leaders". A Frugal Yankee takes advantage of sale items that fit their budget and lifestyle.

Part of this is 'seasonal buying.' As farm production peaks, produce prices drop. The converse is true to a lesser degree in our global economy as the seasons change around the world.

Seasonal buying is an effective way to keep the food budget in line. Getting savvy about what is coming into season helps define the family menu. For example, asparagus in the spring, apples in the fall, cranberries around Thanksgiving.

There are some supermarket tricks when it comes to sales.

SIZE DOESN'T MATTER: Usually the five for $5 sale does not mean you must buy all five to get the special price. It simply means they are a dollar each and buy only what you need. They are trying to get you to buy more.

BOGO a GO-GO: BOGO is an acronym for Buy One, Get One free. Many times prices are jacked up so you get only a small savings.

UNIT PRICING: Unit pricing is the shopper's best friend. It is simple way to find the best value. The cost per unit strips away any pretense found in packaging or marketing. The "giant economy" size may not be the best deal.

Package sizes are often misleading, sometimes on purpose. Serving sizes are unregulated and can be very confusing. While one manufacturer may think a serving is 6 ounces, another uses 8 ounces.

The ubiquitous warning "contents may settle" confuses the issue even more. Package size, settled or not, is not an effective way of assessing value.

It gets more confusing. For example, comparing cereals is dicey. Some are compact and heavy (raisin bran). Some are light and airy (corn flakes). People will ordinarily eat more (by weight) of the heavy one. It makes sense to compare unit prices of various brands of raisin bran, but not to compare unit costs of raisin bran vs corn flakes.

The unit price is THE most effective tool for a shopper, clarifying value and price. It's not smart to automatically buy anything simply based on the lowest unit price. It's just one tool in deciding. A more expensive product may have better ingredients, taste better or be more convenient.

STORE BRANDS: Many store brands are made by brand name manufacturers. They are usually just as good. Savings of 20-40% is not unusual. If there is resistance in your family, don't announce it is a store brand, just break them in slowly.

RAIN CHECKS: If something on sale is not in stock, ask for a rain check. Go to the customer service desk. Don't forget to bring the rain check along next time you shop.

BEYOND SALES: here are a few more saving tricks:

- Find a store that sells day old bread at big discounts. Buy and freeze.
- Look for days when meat departments puts 'manager's specials' out. Usually these are meats with a 'sell by' date. Look at the date, then buy and freeze. Or cook big batches of food, then place in portion controlled plastic ware, then freeze.
- Look for new items with great introductory offers.
- Look for recently discontinued items.

COUPONS

Since the start of The Great Recession, coupon use has increased. Rather than lower prices, manufacturers use them to impel sales. Consumers, not willing to lower their perceived standard of living, use them to maintain that standard.

In 2010, 347 billion coupons were issued, the most in any year. Over 3.4 billion were redeemed, up 27% in two years. Today, as in the past, the majority of coupons are found in Sunday newspaper circulars. Coupons are now found in the numerous online websites. Some ask for personal information, so be leery of them. A good place to start are respected sites like Coupons.com and Smartsource.com.

Using both traditional and new sources, a Frugal Yankee finds $4-$6 worth of useful coupons every week. That's $200 -$300 a year. That makes sense.

DOUBLE COUPONS: Some stores offer double coupons. Most double the value of the coupon up to 99¢. Some have one day a week or the occasional promotion offering double coupons. Explore the possibilities in your area and take advantage of them. It's worth shifting shopping days.

COUPONS PLUS REBATE: One of the best deals out there and it spells "jackpot". It's a coupon for an 'on sale' item that also has a rebate. There is a certain joy that comes when you maneuver the system and get something free or nearly free! Scan weekly circulars, then match sales with coupons.

COUPONS PLUS BOGO: Another is matching up an item that is BOGO (Buy One, Get One free) with a coupon. For example, a store has a BOGO deal on soup.

Buy one can at $2.39, get a second one free. If they also have a double coupon day, then give them a $1 coupon. Bingo! Two cans for $0.39.

COUPONS - FINAL WORD: Coupon clipping can be addictive. Clip only for products you use or you want to try. Develop a system of organization and winnowing expired coupons. Otherwise they will become unwieldy.

COUPONS - THE FUTURE: Coupons and how they are distributed is undergoing tectonic changes. The emergence of smart phones is changing how they are marketed and used.

The Frugal Yankee will explore that in more Detail in our chapter entitled FUTURE (im)PERFECT.

DEFEND YOURSELF

Understanding the ways the food industry tries to manipulate us allows a good defense. Here are few of their tricks.

EYE LEVEL, BUY LEVEL: Eye level is where you look first. Stores have learned that items at eye level sell more, maybe twice as much. Is it any wonder then that it's where they place their most profitable products? Manufacturers pay for this prime real estate knowing it will produce more sales. A corollary to this is that kid's stuff is at their eye level. They hope yammering children pleading for this product or that will force parents to succumb to their nagging entreaties. What's the take away? The more costly foods are at eye level, or at child's eye level for an aisle stocked with kid's food. Obviously deals will seldom be found there.

READING LEFT: Americans read left to right. The same is true in supermarkets. The more expensive products are usually on the left. Put these principles together and you know that eye level, on the left of the section is where the stores want you to buy.

STUCK IN THE MIDDLE : Stores prefer you spend as much time looking for food as possible. They plan the stores accordingly. A simple example of this is that the most popular item in an aisle is in the middle. A customer has to work their way from one end to the other. Maybe they will buy something else as they journey. It's all about temptation.

ENDS JUSTIFY THE MEANS: The rise of discount stores or dollar stores has brought a new wrinkle into the supermarket - end of aisle displays and bin displays.

End of aisle displays are those big stacks of product with blaring signs that say sale.

Bin displays are packages crudely piled on top of one another usually in an open space.

Both play off a perception that these are remainders or big price cuts. Look carefully. In most cases they're not.

IF THEY CUT IT, YOU'LL GET SLICED: Pre-sliced and pre-chopped foods are growing in popularity. It's simple - cut up food costs more, a lot more. The only way a Frugal Yankee should buy chopped veggies is if you have a deep and abiding fear of knives, or if you need a tiny bit of carrot or lettuce and would end up wasting the rest.

Oh, one other thing, baby carrots aren't 'baby carrots'. They are carrots milled to look small. If you buy them you're buying a regular old carrot whittled down. You're paying for the packaging, the waste and the whittling.

Yogurt is on sale, 10 for $5. I only want 5 and I've got a coupon for $1 off 5. I checked to make sure I get the low price with fewer than 10. My 5 cups of yogurt cost 30¢ each. (5 x 50¢ = $2.50; subtract $1 for the coupon; 5 for

DIVIDED WE FALL: Many stores create duplicate sections for items like baked goods, cheese or deli. There are a few reasons for this. Sometimes it is an associative connection. For example, cheese near wine as well as in dairy. Sometimes it is to spur the more casual shopper towards an impulse buy. It is best to stick to the list and avoid over buying.

24

ALL TOGETHER NOW: Foods are grouped for associations that promote impulse buying. For example, chips, soda, popcorn and dips all next to each tempts the eye and the pocket book.

DIVIDE & CONQUER: The opposite of grouping foods is to spread them all over the place, especially staples.

Supermarkets won't make their quarterly profit goals if shoppers stick to buying basics. So these 'must have' foods are spread all over the store with temptations en route. Consider milk is in one back corner while bread is another. Again, promoting impulse buying is the objective.

THE MOVEABLE FEAST: The Frugal Yankee found this in big box warehouse stores more frequently than in supermarkets. Just when you've learned where everything is, the store rearranges. It's part of the plan. If you don't know where it is, you look. You spend more time looking, the chances of impulse buying are increased. Seeing a theme here?

THE STATIONARY FEAST: Cafe, newspapers, fresh coffee and a bakery pumping out enticing aromas, it is all designed to keep the shopper in store longer. The longer the shopper stays the more likely they will fall for the temptations.

A side line to this is those nice people with a hot plate offering free tasty tidbits. Generosity? Hardly. Studies show that when given free food, mouths water, stomachs crave and shoppers buy more. It's not just the food sampled. Something tasty sampled spurs more adventurous shoppers willing to try other, impulse driven, foods.

A Lick of History

S&H Green Stamps and, its rival, Plaid
Stamps were rewards programs for shoppers.
They started in the 1890s and were
effectively over by the 1980s. It was one of
the first loyalty programs. Shoppers were given
stamps based on their purchases. When
enoough stamps were collected, they could be
redeemed for prizes. At one point, the S&H
Catalog was the largest publication in the US
and they printed three times as many stamps
as the US Post Office.

FUTURE (im)PERFECT

Science fiction is taking over your local supermarket. No, it isn't some alien slime wad bent on using humans as pop tarts. It is that as supermarkets continue to aggressively secure market share, they look at and use new technologies. Some of these technologies are amazing and wonderful, but they can also create problems of an imperfect world.

The biggest buzz is NFC, Near Field Chips. Using 'apps' on your smart phone, the phone can do a plethora of tasks, inform, search for coupons, compare prices, act as a debit or credit card, and in some scenarios, talk to your refrigerator. As one

industry executive said, it is all about "creating a personal conversation between the store and the shopper."

Briefly here is a description of some of the new 'toys'.

GEO LOCATOR: Using GPS locators, stores recognize your smart phone as you drive by. They send a text to your phone with a discount designed to lure you in immediately. Talk about capturing an audience! Already a new term has been spawned, geospam.

COMPARISON SITES: Scan an item into the smart phone's bar code app. It will scour the internet for the best deal available and where. Pricing becomes more competitive. Of course, this assumes the problem of maintaining a huge database is solved. Right now there are gaps. It's a tool, not a definitive answer.

SCAN AS YOU GO: Using a smart phone or a store provided hand held device, shoppers scan items as they shop. The app keeps a running total and when shopping is done, a simple swipe at the check out kiosk completes the transaction. Stores and manufacturers are keen on this. While you shop, the wi-fi or NFC component produces coupons for companion items already purchased. It is an updated tool to promote impulse buying.

HIGH TECH COUPONS: The Great Recession taught everyone lessons. Brand name manufacturers learned that coupons allowed them to maintain current pricing but still offer deals. Shoppers can use this and other marketing ploys to their advantage.

Merging smart phones and the web, manufacturers now offer coupons before we shop, while we shop and even as we check out. Their ability to influence sales is enhanced. For consumers, there will be more offers. They trick is NOT to buy things simple because they are on sale. As we said earlier, stick to the list and the budget.

SELF CHECKOUT: This is already well under way. The shopper goes to an automated checkout, scans the item and pays. One employee can handle more customers at a given time. This practice will increase over the next few years especially with NFC and smart phones.

THE FRIDGE THAT CAME OUT OF THE COLD: Computer capable fridges can now create precise cooling areas for specific foods making food last longer. That's just one of the new technologies in the standard ice box. Soon smart phones and fridges will 'talk' to each allowing shoppers to know what is in the fridge, generate a cell phone shopping list and suggest menus.

IT MAKES CENTS

There are people who don't like the bother. They picture hours of effort to save $3 a week. It hardly seems worth it. A Frugal Yankee knows differently. An hour a week plus a few attitudinal changes can yield more than some significant coin.

Let's start with a family that spends $120 a week on food. How much could they save using some of the ideas talked about here? Let's see.

Reducing grocery waste = $18/week

Coupon Savings = $12/week

Stocking up with sales = $8/week

Drop name brands = $5/week

Using unit pricing = $4/week

That's $47. A week. Over the course of a year that's $2,400. Now multiply that by 10 years, and you've paid for one semester of college, albeit a state university. Oh, did you notice, you're eating better, getting healthy and maybe, just maybe, losing some extra poundage.

Follow the simple steps outlined in this book and see what happens. Being a Frugal Yankee at the supermarket can result substantial money savings and health.

In future books, the Frugal Yankee will check out warehouse stores, yard sales, the new coupon boom and the Frugal house.